# How to Organize Your Life to Maximize Your Day

Effective Time Management Tips and

Ideas to Simplify Your Life

Judith Turnbridge

© 2013 Judith Turnbridge

**All Rights Reserved. No part of this publication may be reproduced in any form or by any means, including scanning, photocopying, or otherwise without prior written permission of the copyright holder.**

Disclaimer and Terms of Use: The Author and Publisher has strived to be as accurate and complete as possible in the creation of this book, notwithstanding the fact that he does not warrant or represent at any time that the contents within are accurate due to the rapidly changing nature of the Internet. While all attempts have been made to verify information provided in this publication, the Author and Publisher assumes no responsibility for errors, omissions, or contrary interpretation of the subject matter herein. Any perceived slights of specific persons, peoples, or organizations are unintentional. In practical advice books, like anything else in life, there are no guarantees of income made. This book is not intended for use as a source of legal, business, accounting or financial advice. All readers are advised to seek services of competent professionals in legal, business, accounting, and finance field.

First Printing, 2013

Printed in the United States of America

# Table of Contents

Don't Agonize, Organize ................................................................... 6

What Do We Mean by 'Organized' .................................................. 7

Start to Organize Your Day by Organizing Your Sleep ................ 8

    Following a Bedtime Routine .................................................... 8

        Getting Your Clothes Ready for the Next Day ..................... 9

        How to Organize Your Closet – The Basics .......................... 9

        Get Enough Sleep by Calculating Your "Bedtime Range" ..... 10

        Finding the Best Way to Fall Asleep .................................... 13

    Room Clearing Tips – The Basics! ........................................... 15

Organizing Your Morning Routine ............................................... 18

    The Morning Chill-Out ............................................................. 18

        Organizing Your Chill Space ................................................. 19

    Breakfast the Organized Way! ................................................. 19

        Pre-Plan Your Breakfast ........................................................ 20

    Organizing Your Kitchen Cabinets – The Basics ..................... 22

    Organizing Your Bathroom ....................................................... 23

Organizing Your Work Life ........................................................... 25

    Preparing For Your Journey to the Office ................................ 25

    How to Use Your Commute to Keep Ahead of the Game! ....... 26

How to Organize Your Workspace ......................................................... 29

How to Organize Your Home for Work ................................................. 31

Working in an Organized Manner ........................................................ 33

    Creating a Daily Schedule .............................................................. 33

    Creating a To-Do-List ..................................................................... 36

    Organizing Your Email ................................................................... 37

    Coping with Distractions ............................................................... 38

    Setting Your Reminders ................................................................ 39

    Avoiding the Afternoon Slump ..................................................... 39

Organizing Your Home-Life .................................................................. 41

    Preparing Dinner the Organized Way! ......................................... 41

    The Organized Mealtime .............................................................. 43

    The Organized Grocery Shopper .................................................. 43

    Lunchtime ..................................................................................... 45

Some Nifty Little Tips ........................................................................... 46

And Finally ............................................................................................ 50

About the Author .................................................................................. 51

## Don't Agonize, Organize

I'm not a naturally organized person. But I certainly wish I was! I wasn't born with some "Super-Efficiency" gene that enables me to do 2000 things at once, get everything right the first time, and never get flustered. Nope, that doesn't describe me at all. At the risk of offending creationists, I, like everyone else (well most of us anyway) am a descendant of the Great Ape, a mammal **not** renowned for its organizational abilities. Ask yourself, when was the last time you saw a gorilla with a tidy bookshelf, or a chimpanzee diligently flipping through a Rolodex?

Normally, organization isn't that big of a problem. But sometimes everything just seems to collide all at once; I need to find a babysitter for next Tuesday, pick up my hubby from the airport at six, pay that darn electric bill, bake a cake for Jimmy's birthday, remember not to forget Aunt Ethel's birthday – again, and so on. I'm sure you too have found yourself floundering in an ocean of to-do lists and unfinished business. However, despite my lack of talent, I've learned some very useful tricks over the years that have enabled me to cope with life's little challenges and conflicting priorities, without turning me into a hysterical, quivering block of Jell-O. This book is my attempt to share these tricks with you, and hopefully help you to take back control of your life.

## What Do We Mean by 'Organized'

Before we continue, I'd better clarify what I mean by "organized." In the dictionary, the word organized is defined as *"Having one's affairs in order so as to deal with them efficiently."* In other words, it's getting stuff done without hassle by prioritizing tasks. With that being said, this book does not deal in depth with the subject of decluttering your home, despite the apparent confusion some people appear to have over this topic.

For tips on clearing the mess from your life, why not check out my other Amazon books.

Okay, now I've got that bit of shameless plugging out of the way, let's get organized!

# Start to Organize Your Day by Organizing Your Sleep

This may seem like a funny place to start. But if you really think about it, you can't do anything effectively, let alone prioritize the stuff that life throws at you, if you don't get enough sleep. It's a medical fact that one of the first effects of sleep deprivation is an impaired ability to organize and accomplish ordered tasks. Fortunately, there are many tips you can follow that can help you drift peacefully off into the land of nod, without swallowing a mouthful of pills. I've provided some of these below (tips that is, not pills).

## Following a Bedtime Routine

Following a set routine every time you go to bed will train you mind and body to start winding down as you soon as you begin to prepare for sleep.

What you do and how long you do it for is entirely dependent on what suits you best, but here's an example:

A. Warm a cup of milk.

B. Turn off / unplug everything downstairs (except the fridge).

C. Go upstairs, go to the bathroom, brush your teeth, and so on.

D. Put on your nightclothes, sit in a comfy chair, and read for a bit while drinking your milk.

E. When you start getting drowsy, switch off the bedroom lights, and climb into bed.

One quick thing you should do is to avoid caffeinated drinks, like coffee or tea, as these stimulants will keep you awake. Drink a warm, milky beverage instead. There's one more thing you should add to your bedtime routine...

## Getting Your Clothes Ready for the Next Day

No, I'm not trying to be patronizing by suggesting you lay your clothes out like your mom told you. But it really helps to make sure that what you want to wear is all ready to go. Follow these steps:

A. Pick out your clothes. (Duh!)

B. Check them for stains or rips. Then give them a quick sniff in case any of them made their way back into your closet (instead of the hamper) when they shouldn't have (It happens).

C. Grab the iron and give your clothes a quick press, if needed.

D. Choose your shoes, belts, bags, and any other accessories you may need and make sure it all matches.

E. Transfer your wallet, keys, phone, and other necessities to your pockets if you don't intend on carrying a bag.

While we're on the topic of clothes, it's pretty difficult to find anything matching if the inside of your closet resembles something which has been hit by a tornado. So let's switch to a little advice about how to sort this mess out and keep your closet tidy.

## How to Organize Your Closet – The Basics

Here are some suggestions for how to go about organizing your closet:

A. Take all the clothes out of your closet and put them on your bed or other clean surface.

B. Remove any clothes you don't wear and put them in a "donation box."

C. Grab any off-season items and move them into long-term storage.

D. When you put your clothes back in the closet, be sure that all hangers are facing in. Then, when you wear something, turn the hanger around. Any hangers still facing in after a month should go in the "donation box."

E. Group your clothes together by type. For example, shoes with shoes, socks with socks, shirts with shirts, pants with pants, and so on.

F. Sort each grouped item by color. So put all the black pants together and the white blouses together.

G. Keep the closet floor clear. If you're short of space, put up hooks inside the closet door or use a hanging organizer.

H. Keep two storage bins somewhere in your closet. Use one to store the clothes you rarely wear or have decided to donate to charity. Use the other bin to temporarily store stained or torn items.

I. Once a month, you should clean out these bins and take care of whatever needs to be done with the contents. If you sew, fix the torn items. If not, take them to a seamstress. Take the items in the other box to a donation center.

Even more helpful tips on this subject can be found in my companion book *"How to Declutter Your Home for Simple Living."*

## Get Enough Sleep by Calculating Your "Bedtime Range"

Although it is always best to maintain a regular sleep pattern by waking up at the same time each morning, often this isn't possible. If you work varying shifts, have a new baby, or your neighbors decide to throw parties until 4:00 am, you most likely will have trouble keeping regular sleeping hours. Therefore, you need to plan your sleep within a "bedtime range." Here's how it works:

**Decide on your wake-up time**

The time you wake-up depends on your morning routine. Write down what you do on a typical morning, with estimates for how long it takes you to do each task. For example:

1. 'Chill-time' (more on this later) – 10 minutes

2. Breakfast preparation and eating time for you, your family, dog, etc. – 60 minutes

3. Shower, brushing your teeth, other bathroom rituals, etc. – 30 minutes

4. Getting dressed – 10 minutes

5. Drying hair, brushing and styling hair, applying makeup, etc. – 30 minutes

6. Gathering your belongings and double-checking you've got it all – 5 minutes

7. A final tidy up of the house – 5 minutes

Be generous with your timings so they account for the unexpected (like your car refuses to start or your puppy has decided to leave a present for you on the kitchen floor). Now add up those estimates (in this case two and a half hours) and deduct the result from the time you depart for work or start your daily duties. This should give you a wake-up time. For example, if you need to catch a train at 7:30 am, and your morning routine takes one and a half hours, you'll need to get up at 6:00 am (poor you).

## Work out the minimum amount of sleep you need to feel refreshed

Conventional wisdom suggests eight hours of sleep is the norm, but many people need less and some unfortunate ones need more. On average, about six to seven hours seems to do the trick for most individuals.

## Work out how long it takes you to fall asleep

Obviously, this can vary tremendously depending upon the kind of day you had and if you are feeling relaxed or stressed. But on average, it takes most people about 20 minutes to nod off.

## Deduct all the above from your wake up time

If, for example, you need a *minimum* of seven hours sleep, and it takes you 15 minutes to get ready, that's seven hours fifteen minutes in total. Now deduct your wake-up time of, say, 7:30 am. Therefore, you should be in bed *no later* than 12:15 am.

## Now figure out how much sleep you need when you're really tired

If you're really tired, you might need to adjust your bedtime. By this I mean, if you are so tired it feels like you'd could drop off in the middle of a senten…ZZZZ.

## Next, take this *maximum* sleep figure and adjust it

Considering the maximum amount of time you need to sleep, add on how long it takes you to fall asleep and deduct that from your wake up time.

Building on the earlier example, if after a hectic day you need eight and a half hours sleep, you should go to bed *no later* than 10:45pm to be up and nicely refreshed by 7:30 am.

Voilà! You've just figured out your healthy "bedtime range." Going with the example we've been using, the bedtime range would be from 12:15 am to 7:30 am or 10:45 pm to 7:30 am.

Please note that this strategy merely provides "ballpark" figures. Other things may factor in to the amount of sleep you personally require. This example was not intended to be followed dogmatically.

However, by following a "bedtime range" you have a useful organizational guide for getting enough sleep, as well as the benefit of keeping your mind clear so you are able to prioritize and process the events of the day.

## Finding the Best Way to Fall Asleep

It's great to be able to calculate how much sleep you need, but what if you can't fall asleep in the first place?

There are dozens of books devoted to this subject, and space dictates that I can't cover all of them here. But I will share a few of the best tips I know:

**Wear earplugs**

If you can get used to them, earplugs are about the best sleep aids out there! Avoid the ones for swimmers or those for long flights, because they can cause your ear canals to ache like crazy after a couple of hours. Avoid wax plugs too, as they are virtually useless and yucky to boot! The best types are disposable foam plugs. These can be formed to fit snugly into the ear canal and are so effective that they are often used by industrial workers. If they start to become dirty, though, throw them away to avoid the risk of an ear infection. Also, try to avoid using them every night or else you may promote wax formation in the ear.

**Keep the bedroom dark and quiet**

Whenever possible, close the drapes or blinds to keep light out of the room while you're trying to get to sleep. (Obviously, know where your bedside lamp is, so you can find it by touch if you need light!) Use low-power lamps to maintain a relaxing atmosphere if you need to get up for some reason during the night. If possible, keep windows and doors closed, so as to shut out street sounds. Hang heavy drapes and spread around thick rugs to help combat any disturbances from noises such as wind howls, floorboard creaking, cooling water pipes, and other house settling noises.

**Avoid watching TV or using computers while trying to fall asleep**

Switch off those glowing boxes of wonder and delight as the light from their screens can over-stimulate your brain. When you are mulling over what you've just seen on TV or read on the Internet, it keeps you awake! Stop watching, blogging, and searching at least an hour before you go to bed.

If you have a TV or a computer located in your sleeping area, get them out of there if at all possible. Then, you won't be as tempted to use them. If nothing else, switch the darn things off, unplug them from wall, and hide them out of sight while you're in bed. You'll be surprised on how much better you will sleep after you eliminate some of these distractions.

**Don't take your mobile phone to bed**

Yes, we all have handy-dandy alarms on our cell phones that can wake us by whatever tone we desire. They may gently return us to the conscious realm through the velvet sound of Perry Como's voice, or blast us into action from a 90 second burst of an air-raid siren, but I wouldn't recommend them – buy a proper alarm clock instead.

How many times have you found yourself nicely dozing off only to be startled awake again by a delayed text message, a beep from the "battery charged" indicator, or one of those mysterious "glowing screen for no reason" events? Phones also put your brain into a "waiting for action" mode that you need to avoid if you want to peacefully drift off to sleep.

**Stop working… Period!**

About an hour or so before bedtime, stop doing any work, be it physical or mental. About the most taxing thing you should do (Biblically acceptable that is) is a little light reading. Avoid doing any work at all in the bedroom, as this may "train" your mind to associate this space with activity, rather than restful sleep like it should. If you find anything that reminds you of work, like documents, clip binders, uniforms or your lion-taming chair, take them out the room or store them out of sight somewhere, like in a closet or drawer.

**No snacks before bed**

This tip is so obvious, that it's often ignored! Apart from the old wives tale that eating cheese before bedtime gives you nightmares (which is a bunch of nonsense by the way), the action of laying down encourages gastric juices and any partially digested food to flow back up your alimentary canal. This could potentially choke you, or at the very least give you a nasty case of heartburn. It's therefore important to avoid eating anything at least an hour before you go to bed – even if you're famished!

**One last thing: Tidy up your bedroom**

Apart from providing a sense of "closure" to the day, it also ensures that you wake up to a nice, comforting, and inviting environment. Nobody wants to wake up to a dispiriting pile of clutter that reminds you just how behind you are with your chores!

## Room Clearing Tips – The Basics!

Now that I've mentioned about tidying up, this seems like a good place to share some good advice about it.

– If you're passing through a room and you spot something that should be in another room, stop what you're doing, pick up the offending item, and return it to where it belongs.

– If you're in a room where items belonging to it are out of place, stop what you're doing, and put those items away where they belong.

– If you are about to step over something that doesn't belong there on the floor, stop what you're doing, pick it up, and put it back where it should be.

Can you spot the common theme, here? No? Well let me spell it out to you. If you see something out of place, stop what you're doing, and put it back in the *right place – right now!*

Don't even think about it! Don't give yourself any chance to make some miserable excuse for delaying in cleaning up that room; excuses like "I'm tired," "I'll do it tomorrow," or "I'll do it after *Days of Our Lives* has finished." To quote Elvis Presley, "Tomorrow Never Comes" and you'll soon forget about that mess or even cease to care it's there. Rapidly, the lousy habit of "leaving it till tomorrow" takes over and the mess piles up. Pretty soon, you'll be living in a chaotic mess and buying my books for help!

I call this condition "clutter-blindness" and developing it is as easy as falling off a log. What is "clutter-blindness?" It's a nasty, progressive condition where you become so accustomed to the mess that you're oblivious to it, thus allowing clutter to take over your life. Here's the good news. The cure to "clutter-blindness" is just as easy and very simple to implement! By forcing yourself to act IMMEDIATELY, the minute you see ANY mess, no matter how trivial, you'll gradually reprogram yourself to become "clutter-aware." In no time at all, you will live in that beautiful, tidy oasis you've always dreamed about! (Phew! I think I need a lie down after writing all that!)

**Room Clearing Tips – Even More Basics!**

Now, that I've had a quick nap and an ice-cold shower, here are a few more tips for you regarding the care of the rooms in your house.

– Keep a short, quick list of tasks you need to get done around the house and complete a few each day. Sometimes, despite our best efforts, things get neglected and the chores pile up. Building a simple list, however, will stop you from feeling overwhelmed by the scale of things and allow you to monitor your progress.

– If you find things that just don't belong anywhere or to anyone, get rid of them! NOW! Sell them on the Internet, give them to friends, donate them to charity, or throw them out with the trash. How you get rid of them doesn't matter as much as getting rid of them AS SOON AS YOU CAN! Whatever you do – AVOID HOARDING! In my view, hoarding is just a fancy term for junk-collecting!

– Deal with your snail mail as soon as it arrives; NEVER let it pile up! Apart from being bad for organization, it's terribly messy and makes it even more difficult to pay your bills on time.

Hopefully by now, you've implemented my strategies and had a great nights rest. Now it's time to face the challenges of the day. How we face them is crucial to our success in our quest for an organized existence. Read on and I'll tell you how!

# Organizing Your Morning Routine

## The Morning Chill-Out

As soon as that alarm breaks into life, some people (those of us that are super-human at least) jump straight out of bed and into the shower with admirable efficiency. A lot more, however, simply smack that snooze-button and lie there, half-awake. Then it dawns on them that they have just 10 minutes left in which to get-up, shower, throw on some clothes, gulp down some coffee, and run like hell for the train!

Leaving everything to the last minute is obviously very disorganized behavior and it's a surprisingly difficult habit to break. However, the good news is that lounging about when you first wake up isn't necessarily a bad thing.

The trick is to incorporate your dozing into your morning routine and to use it constructively! I call this my morning "chill-out" time and it works because it allows you to gather yourself and ease into the day rather than frantically throwing yourself into everything. The amount of time you do this is up to you, but I'd recommend "chilling" for at least 10 minutes. I would stress, however, that you do something that you can't do in bed (apart from the obvious, like using the bathroom).

Chill-out time ensures you won't fall back to sleep again. It also helps you to build an association in your mind between your chill-time and waking up. Do something that's relaxing and enjoyable, such as reading a chapter from your favorite book, meditating, or saying a prayer, if you're so inclined. Sitting quietly in a darkened room, listening to the clock ticking away is also perfectly acceptable.

Stretching exercises or practicing yoga is great to do while chilling, as both activities prepare both your mind and body for the day ahead. Avoid watching the TV, listening to the radio, getting dressed, or eating breakfast; remember your day hasn't officially started yet – you're just getting ready for it!

## Organizing Your Chill Space

If you can, do your chilling away from your bedroom; that way you won't be tempted to crawl back into bed! It also maintains your mind's association between your bedroom space and sleep. It's important to understand that one of the keys to becoming organized is to decide the purpose of each room in your house and use them solely for that purpose. For example, bedrooms are for sleeping in, not for watching TV. Meanwhile, the living room is for watching TV, not sleeping.

Choose a chill-area that is appropriate for your tasks and for quietly relaxing – deciding to meditate in the garage is probably not a good idea.

Most importantly, always keep your chill-space tidy and clutter free. If we clear all our living spaces as we use them, we can then organize our environment with very little effort!

Now that we've gotten up and done our stretching exercises during chill-time, hopefully, we feel ready to face the day and handle the challenges ahead. However, you won't be very effective running around on an empty stomach. It's now time to prepare the most important meal of the day: Breakfast!

## **Breakfast the Organized Way!**

How many times, have you grabbed that box of cereal, poured some into a bowl, thrown away the annoying little plastic toy that fell out, then gone over to the fridge, taken out the milk, only to find it smells like month-old yogurt? Maybe you should have checked it out previously! Maybe you WILL in the future…

## Pre-Plan Your Breakfast

Get into the habit of planning your breakfast the day before. Each night before you go to bed, check to make sure you have all the ingredients you will need in the morning. If not, you can run to the store (if it's not too late) or you can adjust your selection. Do this even if you're only planning to eat something as straightforward as toast. You don't need to have a super comprehensive menu stuck to your fridge door, just quickly review that you have all the components and they are all fresh and ready to go. You always want to have a good, organized start to your day.

### Stick to a Regular, Daily Menu

This saves a lot of hassle and stops you from turning into a short order chef every morning. Say good-bye to running yourself ragged at the mercy of other people's breakfast whims! Although, eating the same things most days may sound a little boring, you can vary things by changing your menus periodically – say once a week, while providing additional choices for the weekends. By sticking to a regular breakfast menu, you can plan your shopping way ahead of time, and save money by purchasing the ingredients you need in bulk.

### Clean Up Afterwards

Even if all you had for breakfast was a cup of coffee, clean it up immediately when you've finished. Another key to getting organized is to deal with chores as you go; it takes far less effort to manage many little tasks than one big one. Try to avoid letting dirty dishes pile up in the sink!

### Organizing Your Refrigerator

In the morning, the last thing you need is to rummage around in the fridge only to find you've run out of eggs, or someone has sneakily used up the rest of the bacon for a midnight feast. And nobody wants to find that their bread has turned a lovely shade of emerald green!

To make sure you never have to eat dry cornflakes again, try the following useful tips for organizing the contents of your fridge:

– Clear out old or stale food. Not only is this good for the pallet, it's good for your health, too! No matter how thoroughly you clean them, harmful germs can thrive in the fridge and grow on your food!

– Group similar items together, such as keeping all your condiments in one part, all your juices in another, and so on.

– Use the drawers the way they were intended. Fruit and vegetables go in the lower drawers and cold-cuts, deli stuff and cheese go in the middle ones.

– Place your taller items in the appropriate spot and on the correct shelf. If your fridge has only one large shelf, put the tallest items, like soda bottles and wine bottles, near the back so you won't knock them over as you reach in for other items. You certainly don't want to inadvertently spray your kitchen floor with sticky pop!

– Store as much as you can in microwavable, transparent containers. Not only can this keep your food fresh and restrict the spread of germs, it allows you to see food options at a glance. Leftovers provide you with instant, home-prepared, ready-made meals that can be popped straight into the microwave when needed!

– Keep your refrigerator no more than two-thirds full. This allows you to see everything and restock more effectively. This will not only help you to waste less food, but you'll also be able to locate items more easily.

– Before each trip to the grocery store, thoroughly check out what's already in your fridge. This will keep you from doubling up on items and also remind you about food that should be thrown away.

## Organizing Your Kitchen Cabinets – The Basics

The task of organizing your kitchen cabinets can seem overwhelming at times, and this is especially true when we consider the huge array of items often stored there. For many of us, the lack of space means our kitchen cabinets can literally be bursting at the seams. So, there's only one thing to do and that's roll up our sleeves and bring order to the chaos.

I am going to share with you the basics regarding how to organize your cabinets:

a) Store all your similar items together, i.e. cups with cups, plates with plates, knives with knives, and so on.

b) Install some shelf organizers, such as plate racks or cutlery trays. Not only will these keep things together, they'll save an awful lot of cupboard space too.

c) Get rid of anything that isn't used regularly. Likewise, only keep the minimum of what you need and be ruthless about what you throw out. Ask yourself: is it really necessary to have four pizza cutters? Are you ever going to use that day glow orange fondue set given to you as a wedding present back in 1973? If the answer is no – throw it away! If it is yes and I were you, I'd at least give it a thorough wash before dipping anything in that fondue pot ever again!

d) Store items near where you use them. For example, keep pots and pans next to the stove and glasses close to the refrigerator or sink. Use your common sense when you are organizing and deciding what goes with what. It would be really unwise to store kitchen paper next to your gas range. If you make a poor decision like that, you may encounter undesirable results and subsequently face involuntary manslaughter charges for killing someone in a fire!

e) Put the items you use the least towards the back of the cupboards and place the ones you use the most often at the front, within easy reach. If you want to be really organized, keep a list handy of where you've stored all your least assessable items, so you won't need to rummage through everything in order to find them again.

Okay, now we're done talking about organizing those kitchen cupboards. "But, what about those cabinets in the bathroom?" I hear you cry. So, without further ado, let's move on.

## Organizing Your Bathroom

When organizing your bathroom, here are few ideas for you to consider:

a) Keep only medicines in the medicine cabinet. This advice may seem so obvious that it's almost patronizing. But, it's amazing to learn how many cosmetics, toiletries, and other bits of junk can wind up in these cabinets. Remember to throw out any creams or medications that are past their expiration date. It's surprising how many of these medicines need to be replaced within a year of purchase. Make sure to check those "use by" dates regularly. Only keep what is necessary too, as not only will it allow you to keep on top of what you have, it will also save you a ton of space.

b) If you don't have a proper medicine cabinet, then buy one! Not only will this help you organize your medicines, it will also ensure nasty accidents don't happen by mixing up similarly packaged bathroom products and cosmetics with potentially dangerous medications. If you can, buy a cabinet that is lockable to prevent your kids from getting into your medicine.

c) Throw out any bathroom clutter. Only store the soaps, perfumes, and toiletries you need. Throw out any that are old or rarely used. Be particularly ruthless with all of those redundant toiletry sets given to you by unimaginative relatives as Christmas gifts. Alternatively, do the unthinkable and actually use them up before you buy any more!

e) Use a shower caddy. This allows you to put all your shower items together and keep them conveniently at hand. As with the medicine cabinet, only store what you need in the caddy.

d) Group similar cosmetic products together in individual make-up bags or small containers. For example, you could your keep hair care products and brushes in a bag, your nail polishes in a clear plastic container, and all your lipsticks together in a separate box.

By now you should have devised some nicely organized sleeping and morning routines. If not go back and quit skipping chapters, you lazy thing!

# Organizing Your Work Life

There's a heavy hint in the heading regarding the purpose of this chapter. And no, it's not about pet care, smarty pants – it's about how to organize your work day.

This section assumes you work in an office that you need to commute to, but if you work from home, you'll find plenty of useful tips here as well.

## Preparing For Your Journey to the Office

Like everything else about organization, pre-planning is the key to success! The more relaxed and together you are when you walk in, the better. That means making sure you're not rushing around at the last minute, frantically tearing the place apart looking for your keys, your mobile phone, or purse. Not to mention being oblivious to the fact that you managed to tuck your blouse into the back of your panties while attempting to apply lipstick and throwing your clothes on at the same time. So, here are a few tips to avoid that pre-commute panic!

– Lay out your clothes, bags, keys, and everything else you need, the night before you leave. If you tend to take the same things to work with you daily, lay them out in the same place, as soon as you *come in* from work each evening. That way they are ready to be picked up when you leave the next day, rather than having to try to remember that you left them in a disorganized heap on the dining room table!

– Keep a list of the things you need to take with you in your purse (provided you don't lose that too), and check it again just before you leave. Alternatively, tape this list at eye-level to the inside of the door by which you leave, if you're particularly absent minded.

– Check the gas levels in your car and fill it up if necessary. If you use public transportation, be sure you have all the train or bus tickets you need to get to work and home again or at least have the cash to purchase them. Check these things the night *before* and preferably during your journey home. The goal is for these procedures to become part of your working routine and get you into the daily habit of doing them. Moreover, doing these checks beforehand helps you to classify your day into work and downtime. This enables you to 'switch off' from the office during your leisure periods, which is great for combating stress as well as recharging your inner battery!

– Learn a few alternate routes to work so you can avoid traffic jams or disruption from road construction. Likewise, do the same for bus and train journeys in case of timetable disruptions. Even if it takes a little longer than usual, at least you'll be moving!

– Get into the habit of checking your train company's websites for any planned engineering work that may disrupt your journey. Be particularly diligent during the winter months. This allows you to make alternative arrangements or warn your employer of when you maybe late for work (you may even get into their good graces for doing this).

– Try carpooling, so you can get a little extra work done while you're being taken to the office.

– Always, always leave early, by at least 10 minutes. As a rule of thumb, add about 15-20 percent to your journey time, so hopefully you can deal with most of the unexpected eventualities you may encounter (bar alien abduction or your credit card being swallowed up by a faulty ticket machine).

## How to Use Your Commute to Keep Ahead of the Game!

For many of us that trip to work is dead time. We just sit there (that is, if you're lucky enough to even get a seat in the first place), for what seems like an eternity, vegetating on the train, subway, or bus waiting for the doors to open so we can stagger out, in a daze, towards yet another day of work. But, it doesn't have to be like that; we can use this time to mentally prepare ourselves for work, or perhaps even do a little work while we were on the move. What you do while you're commuting depends on your method of transport. The various transportation methods are covered below.

– If using a carpool or traveling by public transportation:

If you have the space, break out that laptop! Some trains even have free Wi-Fi available so you can access the Internet and use your time constructively by checking your emails before you arrive at the office. Unless, you actually need it for work, DON'T login to Facebook, Twitter, Linkedin or any other social media sites or you'll end up wasting your time by doing something worthless instead. There's no need to be watching skateboarding dogs on YouTube or spending 20 minutes tending to a virtual farm when you could be doing something productive instead.

If you are answering emails, you may be crunched for time, so you will need to prioritize them and reply to the ones that require the shortest answers first. (I cover how to deal with email in more detail, later in this book.)

If you can't access your email account, there are plenty of other tasks, such as working on documents, spreadsheets, or presentations, while using your laptop.

If you can't use your computer, then why not do a little work-related reading instead. Some ideas are browsing through any trade journals or magazines you might have, reviewing technical documents, or maybe even scouring the newspapers for a job that's closer to home!

One great thing you could do is write out a to-do list for the day (there's more about these later, too).

Another great tip is to do the things you like the least during your journey. If you hate wading through sales statistics, take a deep breath and fire up that spreadsheet! If composing best practice procedures for widget storage bores you into a coma, force yourself to open that pesky document and start typing away. Because you will be limited to the travel time it takes you to get to work, you'll be forced to labor for only a tolerably short period of time while having to focus on the very things you'd normally avoid and leave to the last minute. Also, by getting the nasty stuff out of the way, you will face the rest of the day, feeling unburdened and brimming with a sense of achievement. All this and you haven't even got to work yet!

– If you drive:

Obviously, you can't open your laptop or read a technical paper while at the wheel, but there's still plenty you can still do that won't be too distracting and cause you to wreck your car!

If you have a hands-free set, you can use it to make calls and free up other parts of your day. But remember, as with all the tips in this section, make sure you are not distracted from the road!

See if you can, get a "talking book" version of whatever journals you may need to read. You can load them onto your mp3 player or burn them to CD, then play them back via the car's sound system as you drive. Avoid earphones though, as it is dangerous not to be able to hear what's happening around your vehicle while you are driving.

Recite to yourself any speeches or important conversations you might need to give or have at work. Want a piece of advice? Try not to do this with too many people watching or else they might think you've turned into a loony!

If nothing else, you can start to think about the day ahead and mentally prepare for it. You could also contemplate your to-do list. You can then dictate any ideas or thoughts you might have into a voice recorder. Most cell phones have this option, but make sure you use hands-free sets and, as I said earlier, make sure you're not distracted from driving your car.

– If you walk or ride your bicycle to work:

All the stuff you can do while driving you can do on your bike or on foot. In fact, it's much safer to do these while walking (unless you're crossing a road). These tasks can also provide a great way for passing the time. If you are practicing a speech, while walking, say it "in your head," or else...well you should remember what others will think. If not, go back a few paragraphs and you'll find out.

## How to Organize Your Workspace

If you managed to get any work done on your trip to work, you're probably already doing better than most of your colleagues. Unfortunately, all those little victories will be eclipsed by the crushing defeat of a desk that resembles the aftermath of a gas explosion at a paper factory. Further humiliation may be inflicted if your filing is so poorly organized that it could be used as supportive examples for the "Chaos Theory."

Having a disorganized working environment may not only greatly hinder your ability to accomplish the tasks required of you, it will give your boss, your clients, and your co-workers the impression that you're inefficient or even incompetent.

An organized workspace is therefore essential to leave the impression that everything is under control. So, let's grab the waste bin, open those drawers, and clean out that desk!

– Clear out any old files and paper correspondence you no longer need. Make sure you understand your employer's policies about how long you need to keep files before you can dispose of them and how they should be destroyed.

– Use your in and out boxes exactly as intended. It's so easy to be tempted to stuff everything willy-nilly into every little nook and cranny if desk space is tight. Or sometimes we don't feel we have the time to sort through our correspondence thoroughly. But, the quickest way to become overwhelmed is by losing track of things. Worst case scenario, you could even be fired if you were to misplace or lose crucial documents!

– Keep the top of your desk almost completely clear. All you need is a computer, an inbox, a notepad, pen and maybe a coffee mug with your name on it! Not only will this provide you with enough space to work, it will also give the impression that you are on top of things (and not that you have nothing to do, as one of my work colleagues believed many years ago. She was fired for losing a company invoice by the way). I'd therefore recommend you that you keep staplers, hole punchers, paperclips, pens, and other supplies in a lockable drawer, which also stops them from being, ahem, "permanently borrowed" by your co-workers.

– Keep only the items you use regularly close by. These can be stored in the upper drawers of your desk, and everything else can be put further away, such as in the lower drawers.

– Use containers and desk organizers intelligently. Your pens should be in a drawer organizer and not rolling around at the bottom of it. Your inbox should be an actual physical box or tray, not a simple vaguely allocated patch on your desktop. I wouldn't bother either with stacking tray sets, as they are very inflexible space wise and can encourage document stuffing.

If you genuinely don't have the opportunity to file stuff right away, put the document in a "to be filed" box. Make sure it's relatively small and, as it fills up, put it right in front of you, preferably in a slightly annoying spot! That way you cannot merely dump stuff into it and ignore it for long stretches of time! When the box is full, stop everything, put the documents away properly, then move the box to a less conspicuous spot on your desk.

Get some form of calendar or planner and use it diligently. An electronic or good old-fashioned paper one, will suffice, but make sure you can simply and quickly add entries to it. Some software solutions are so cumbersome that they can actually be off-putting to use.

Group items that are similar or related together. Keep pens with pens, staplers with staples, pencils with pencil sharpeners, and so on. Then reserve a special spot (a desk organizer, box, or tray) in your desk to keep each group separated and organized.

Use a bulletin board. You can use an old-fashioned corkboard/bulletin board or a modern magnetic wipe board – the choice is yours! But to get the most out of them, it's a good idea to create sections in order to prevent your board from resembling an early Jackson Pollock within a week, and so becoming impossible to fathom. Label each section in a way that can help you with your 'work flow', such as "To Do," "To Call," "To Arrange," and "Other." This will allow you to organize any notes as you make them. Consequently, you will be able to easily refer back to these notes while you are on the phone.

Make sure you always have a pad of sticky notes and a pen next to your phone, so you can scribble out messages right there and then. As soon as you've finished the call, stick the note straight onto your bulletin board in the appropriate section, so you won't forget about it.

## How to Organize Your Home for Work

Working from home is great isn't it? No commute, no fares, no annoying work colleagues, and no feeling trapped in a stuffy office with the boss breathing down your neck. At least that's the theory; in practice it can take tremendous disciple just to keep working and ignore the distractions. It's therefore vital to maintain a sense of structure to your day, rather than drifting about drinking coffee and watching soaps all day.

But there are some strategies you can implement to stay on task and get your work done. Make sure you get up and go to bed at precisely the same time you would if you worked in an office 30 minutes away. This may sound harsh, but you will need this discipline to avoid falling into the habit of getting up at midday, and working through the night. As a primate designed to labor during daylight hours, this behavior will do your mind and body no good at all, and it will put you badly out of step with everyone else around you.

Next, clearly delineate your working hours from leisure time. If you mix these up, you'll mix up your body and mind, too. Then you'll never get anything done effectively. You can do several things to achieve this separation between work time and play time:

– Reserve a desk solely for work and don't keep any personal stuff on it. If you don't have the space for or can't afford to purchase a separate desk, clear an existing desk of all personal items each morning and prepare it for work. Make this part of your morning routine. At the end of the day, clear away your work and return the personal stuff. When not in use, keep all your work items in clearly labeled boxes so you can speedily set up the desk again the next time you need it. Make sure to keep all personal and work items separated and organized accordingly.

– If you're lucky enough to afford one, buy or designate a second computer (or laptop) specifically for work. If this isn't possible, setup a user ID that's dedicated solely for work on your existing machine. In either case, always keep your professional data separate from your personal files on an external drive and back that up regularly. Alternatively, you could back up your data onto the Internet via "Dropbox" or "Google Cloud," if confidentiality is not a concern. However, be aware that the web is a public network and therefore inherently insecure. Just be careful what you put up there!

– Face a wall or window, so you won't be distracted by what's in the room (like that crack in the ceiling that's just appeared or that horrid spider crawling across floor).

– Send all incoming landline and cell phone calls straight to voicemail. Avoid making any personal calls until break times unless absolutely necessary.

– Clearly label all your boxes, files, and everything else (except the dog, of course). Organize as though your boss or most important client could walk in at the drop of a hat and cast their critical eyes upon you.

## Working in an Organized Manner

This section deals with the wonderful world of paid employment, be it working from home or the office, and how to cope with the daily grind. It is not about working in a particularly tidy country house. Geddit?

### CREATING A DAILY SCHEDULE

Setting a schedule is crucial to organizing your work day; it's like drafting a magic map that guides you through the order in which to do things. Even though unexpected crises and various interruptions can disrupt your plan, a carefully thought out schedule may still help your day to run smoothly and without too much hassle. Below are some tips to help you devise your own schedule:

– Check your work email. Even though you might have done so already on your journey in, always recheck it as soon as you get to the office. Murphy's Law dictates that a vitally important message warning you that your 12:30 pm meeting has been rescheduled to 10:00 am will pop into your inbox during the time it took you to leave your mode of transportation and sit down at your desk. Situations like this happen all the time!

Now, some people say you shouldn't do this as opening your email first thing in the morning may drag you into hours of lengthy, unproductive correspondence that can divert your attention from more pressing matters. This shouldn't be a problem, though, if you are organized. You just need to know how to prioritize your replies and phrase your responses accordingly.

When dealing with email, only reply to the quick and easy ones for now and flag the rest as follow-ups. As a rule, if any message is going to take longer than 10 minutes to answer, it should be left until later.

– Update your to-do list. Once you've dealt with the simple emails, open your to-do list, and add a brief reminder about all those troublesome follow-ups!

– Make your phone calls – now! Remember, the telephone is by far the most direct method of telecommunication there is and so it's the hardest to ignore. Things tend to get done much more quickly over the phone, too. So it's actually a really good idea to get your calls out of the way once you've updated your to-do list. It will also help you to not avoid making calls to your more, shall we say, 'challenging' clients.

– Get on with the big stuff. Once you've made your calls, it's time to tackle some of your bigger projects. Choose a few that will take no more than half an hour to do. If you know you can't finish them within a few hours, then work on each one for about an hour. One method to keep yourself from becoming overwhelmed by work is to break down your projects into easily digestible chunks and then 'peck' away at each bit (yes, I am hungry while writing this).

Avoid developing a 'tunnel vision' approach to work as this will cause some projects to flounder, while others will be over delivered. By following a more effective 'break-it-up' approach, you will also be looking at your work through 'fresh eyes' when you return to your projects. Often, you will spot silly errors and will appraise what you've done more critically and accurately by doing this. You can apply this approach to any sized project, be it a design for a mighty space rocket or for clearing out old clothes from your dressers!

While plowing through your big projects, answer any emails on your to-do-list that are relevant to your projects.

– Recheck your emails again! After you've spent a couple of hours on the big stuff, go back and recheck your email. As before, only answer any new quick-to-reply messages and add the tougher ones to the end of your to-do list.

– Grab some lunch. After all that, it must be time to take a break and munch on some food. It's always a good idea to take at least a five minute break away from your desk every couple of hours, so as to get a bit of a stretch, to let the fresh air clear your head, and to rest your eyes from your computer.

– Do your quick projects. After lunch, grab your to-do list, pick the smallest five or six items, and work on them until completion. When finished, remember to check them off the list. This may include the emails you flagged earlier.

– Recheck you emails again! It's the same deal as before, only do the easy ones and mark the rest as follow-ups and add those to your to-do list.

– Make your afternoon telephone calls. By splitting the times you do them into morning and afternoon rounds, you allow yourself the chance to catch people who work different hours or live in different time zones than you.

– Work on one last big project. If you have the time, grab another 'biggie' and work on that for an hour or so; that way you won't be dragged into working late finishing a smaller project.

– Do a FINAL email check. As soon as you're done reading and answering emails, turn off that darn computer! This will stop any temptation to do a little extra work on something and also prevent you from getting lost in time while playing solitaire or surfing the Internet!

– Redo your to-do-list. Don't know how? Then read on to the next section, the cunningly titled, "Creating a To-Do-List!"

## CREATING A TO-DO-LIST

Ah, the to-do list! Not having one of these is like drinking soup with a fork, knitting a blanket with boxing gloves on, juggling chainsaws while blindfolded, or trying to fathom Windows 8! In no time at all, you'll be floundering about, wasting your efforts on unimportant tasks while neglecting the important things that you need to do. Then, you'll be unable to figure out what to do next. Finally, totally overwhelmed and unable to cope, you could find yourself out of a job and drawing social security or applying for unemployment!

As you might have gathered by now, drafting a to-do list is pretty important! Though writing one is easy, you just need to follow a few golden rules for these to be effective, as explained below:

1) Grab a piece of paper and a pencil. You could also open a spreadsheet or blank document if preferred. But remember that electronic organizers can be unwieldy to use and you can't fold your laptop and put into your wallet (at least not at the time of this writing).

2) Think carefully about everything that needs to be done the next day. Include everything from the smallest little task to the biggest imaginable one. This will serve as your 'working' list for now.

3) As mentioned earlier, break down your big projects into lots of little tasks or things that could be completed within one or two days.

4) Browse your emails to look for anything that you might have missed. Add them to your to-do list.

5) If you have a telephone log, repeat Step 4.

6) Now, prioritize each item on the list by marking numbers next to them. Make #1 your highest priority. For a spreadsheet, this is simply a case of entering numbers into a new column adjacent to your tasks. But if you're using paper, remember to write the numbers down in pencil in case you change your mind about the importance of one of your tasks.

7) Write out the prioritized list. Grab another sheet of paper and copy over all the entries in your 'working' list in descending priority order. Alternatively use the sort facility on your spreadsheet to reorder your entries.

8) Now you have drafted a 'master' list. Next, grab another sheet of paper, or open a new spreadsheet tab and mark it with today's date. Think carefully about what items on your list are *realistically* attainable today. Be honest with yourself here and factor in unexpected interruptions. To put it another way, make sure you're not trying to bite off more than you can chew! Next, select and copy those items to the new sheet or tab. Order them by the priorities you assigned them earlier and transfer the smaller tasks from your big projects on to the list. Put your original 'master' to the side for now.

9) Tackle the tasks on your new 'action' list by priority order and cross them off as you complete them.

10) During the day you may encounter new tasks. Add them to your 'action' list and prioritize them later.

## ORGANIZING YOUR EMAIL

Email is now the standard of modern correspondence and has completely usurped good ol' snail mail for most things. It can also generate just as much of a chaos as a pile of moldy old papers, if you don't organize it properly. Moreover, you use email information to update your to-do list, so it better be right!

– Organize your emails into folders. Don't get too specific when naming them; use the same labels you'd use for your physical files as a guide.

– As soon as you've dealt with your email, get into the habit of filing them immediately into the relevant folder. Don't let them languish in your "inbox" waiting to be buried under a pile of new messages.

– Flag your emails systematically. Color-coding is great for this. For example, red for 'Do It Now,' orange for 'Do It Today,' yellow for 'Do Within a Week,' and so on.

– Keep only the latest version. If your email is part of a chain, often the entire correspondence is incorporated into the replies. So try to keep only the latest version of it to avoid confusion and make the message easier to find.

– Throw out the trivial! I'm not just talking spam here, I mean all those cute little, 'Thank you' emails, or boring newsletters you never read. In a nutshell, if you can't be bothered to read it – trash it!

– Only look at your mail at the set times on your schedule. If you're constantly checking your inbox, you'll never get any work done. There's no shame in having loads of unchecked messages because it's a sign you're getting on with what's more important. Remember to switch off that annoying email alarm thingy; it will tempt you to take a peek into your inbox when you don't need to.

## COPING WITH DISTRACTIONS

No matter how well we plan ahead and organize things, distractions will try to veer us off track. However, you can use the following methods to cope with distractions in an effective way:

– Follow that schedule! If you've written it correctly you should have factored in some breaks anyway.

– Avoid Facebook, Twitter, and other social networking sites (unless it's part of your work). It's the biggest single waste of time there is and if your IT department is on top of things, they will log how much time you've been spent using it. This could get you into a whole heap of trouble!

– Stand up and stretch at least once every hour. Get up from your desk, take a good stretch, and then sit back down again to give your spine, neck, and eyes a rest. This will help reenergize you and break the tedium!

– Don't skip breaks. Even if you feel you don't one, step away from your desk for ten minutes every two hours or so.

– If you work from home, turn off the TV! If you like the radio, listen only to music. Keep it low and keep it instrumental, or else you may be distracted by the lyrics.

## Setting Your Reminders

Reminders are crucial for keeping track of things, especially if you're not blessed with a naturally acute sense of timing, like me! At the start of the day, right after you've done your to-do-list, set the reminders in your electronic calendar to alert you of meetings, when to move to the next phase of your schedule, when to take breaks, and various other important times of your day.

## Avoiding the Afternoon Slump

For many of us, the afternoon is the time of day you pretend to do stuff while waiting to go home. This is entirely natural, actually. Before the invention of artificial light, our prehistoric-selves could only work during daylight hours and so they would begin to wind down a few hours before sunset. Unfortunately, we no longer have that luxury, so here are a few tips to stop you from nodding off at your keyboard after lunch:

– Follow your schedule; it's there to help you keep going.

– Eat a light lunch and avoid alcohol! Pretty obvious, really!

– Avoid drinking too much coffee or tea. This will help you avoid the infamous 'caffeine-crash' that occurs within an hour or so of your previous 'fix.'

– Pick your most interesting tasks for the afternoon. Do the tedious ones in the morning.

– Keep stretching. Also, if you're starting to doze off, take a brisk stroll outside. Even walk around the block to clear your head.

– Never hold meetings or presentations in the afternoon. Though you may have a big audience appreciative of the chance to get away from the desk, most will also be half asleep by the time you've finished and probably won't get much out of it.

– Plan outings. If you have any off-site duties, schedule them for the afternoon. Not only will you have a chance to take a breath of fresh air, you won't be around for others to force work on you at the last minute. If you're lucky, you may even be able to go straight home afterwards!

– Clean up and get comfortable when you arrive home. Take a shower or even a bath when you get home and then slip into clean clothing. You should even do this if you're working at home. Apart from washing the daily grime away, it will relax you and tell your mind and body that your work is over for the day.

## Organizing Your Home-Life

Before I get into the nitty-gritty of dealing with the home, here are a few tips you can apply to any situation:

– Use the times when you're unrushed to prepare for the times when you are. Now, you're probably thinking "What planet is she on? When do I ever have five minutes to spare?" But, you know that's not entirely true. There are always relatively slow periods of your day, even if they are only brief. Use these times to gain time for later.

– Constantly think of ways you can combine related tasks. By doing this, you can do them together or in succession, and thus save time. For instance, try buying replacement stamps at the post office as you're posting that parcel for work. Or stop at the gas station to fill your car on the way to or from work.

– Always prepare in advance. A little work ahead of time can save an awful lot of work in the future!

– If you find you're running behind schedule, don't panic! Just explain the situation if needed and make up the time later when you can.

## Preparing Dinner the Organized Way!

When you stagger through the front door, tired after a hard day, the last thing you want to do is to cook an extravagant dinner for yourself or the family. If you have kids, this can be a particularly demoralizing job. One minute your little bundles of joy are crazy for 'Alphabetti Spaghetti,' the next minute they'll just sit there staring at the plate as if the food is about to eat them!

It's so easy just to order takeout or grab a ready-made meal from the freezer, but I'd resist the temptation if I were you – this is a bad habit to get into! These are very, very expensive ways of feeding yourself and the family. Even worse, they are often full of nasty trans-fats, sugars, and artificial additives that are bad for your health and your waistline.

Most of the time, you'll have no option but to prepare something from scratch. The good news is, by organizing your mealtimes at least you can ease the burden. Here are some ideas:

**Make easy choices**

– Stick to simple recipes with few ingredients. Choose dishes that are a cinch to prepare and quick to cook, like chicken breasts, pasta dishes, stir fries, or maybe even salads, if the kids will eat them.

**Batch cook on the weekends**

– Cook a batch of meals over the weekend and stick individual portions in the freezer. Then they are easy to reheat when needed. Chili dishes, casseroles, pasta sauces, soups, and meatloaf are great for this.

**Prepare ahead of time**

– Cut up your vegetables the night before you cook them and keep them in the fridge in a plastic container. Use labor-saving devices to do the chopping if you're not great with a knife. You don't need to buy anything fancy or even electrically driven; I often use a hand powered plunger-type food chopper that works wonders.

– Freeze pre-cooked rice and pasta then reheat later. Great for stir fries and as the perfect accompaniment to your pre-cooked frozen sauces!

– Take the things you need to defrost for the following day, and move them from the freezer to the refrigerator the night before.

– Have a leftover night. Not only does this save time, money, and waste, but it also saves you from cooking a night or two of the week.

– Have regular meals on regular nights. For instance, you could have pot roast on Monday and spaghetti on Tuesday. You could even do takeout once every other week as a treat.

– Use a slow cooker. This is great for preparing meals in advance, and it permeates the house with lovely smells too!

## The Organized Mealtime

To organize your eating experience, routine is the key!

– Avoid TV dinners! Not only is this bad for family unity, it also gets you into bad eating habits, which then promotes "grazing" and snacking during the day.

– Always eat in your dining area at a proper table. This builds a communal spirit within your family and allows everything to be dealt with within a single allotted time period.

– Always eat at the same time; (see above) this stops you turning into a short-order cook each evening!

– Always clear everything and do the dishes as soon as you've finished your meal. Get into the mindset that dinner isn't over until you've done the chores. You can even get your kids to help you, if they are old enough. This will instill good habits in them early on.

## The Organized Grocery Shopper

All this talk of an organized dinner is academic if you're constantly buying stuff you don't need because it looks like a bargain, or you forget to buy the basics and you are forever dashing out to the nearest

7-Eleven. Here are a few simple tips which will hopefully alleviate these and other such problems:

– Plan your shopping at least a week ahead and always make a list.

– Rotate the same list over and over, only adding to it or altering it periodically.

– Don't buy stuff that's on sale if it's not on your shopping list. You'll easily end up with items you won't need. Eventually you'll waste these items or wind up diverting from your routine menu just to use them.

– Order groceries online. By its very nature, you'll need to make a regular shopping list and be informed of any sales relevant to you. And, of course, you'll save an awful lot of time not standing in the checkout lines!

– Shop alone, if possible. This might not be an option if you have kids, but by going to the store alone, you can focus on the shopping and get it done more quickly (hopefully).

– Shop early in the morning. If you get to the store as soon as it opens, it'll normally be less crowded and you can get out quicker. You'll also find it will be better stocked.

– Set a standard day and time for shopping each week. You can then make this a part of your regular routine.

– Go to the store only once. If you find yourself short of something, make do with what you have. Don't go rushing out again unless it is absolutely necessary.

– Write your list on the back of an envelope and keep any coupons in it. That way you won't lose them.

– You'll need a pen to mark items off the list as you grab them. Keep this in the envelope too so you won't lose it.

– Stick a list of your fridge's contents to its door, so you can add items on your shopping list as you run out.

– When visiting the store, shop the aisles first. Always walk the perimeter last because that's where the fresh or frozen produce is usually kept; that way you'll reduce the time it takes you to get your cold stuff into your fridge or freezer before they start defrosting or going stale.

## Lunchtime

Much of what I've said earlier about food preparation applies here too.

There's one caveat, however; never prepare lunch during weekday mornings as this may badly derail your routine. Always make your lunch preparations the previous evening. It shouldn't take you long to cut up any fruits or veggies, or pack your leftovers. If you have kids, then make their sandwiches the night before as well. Label each child's lunch with their name. Always store lunches in clear-plastic containers or labeled bags in the refrigerator to keep them fresh overnight. That also makes them easy to grab the next morning.

# Some Nifty Little Tips

This section is just a bunch a useful tips you can use to help organize your life.

**Figure out the three most important tasks for the day**

Write down and make a mental note of these things as soon as you wake up in the morning. By doing this, you'll get some of your more worrisome tasks out of the way and you will often find that everything else simply falls into place.

**Don't get bogged down with gadgets!**

Today, we are simply surrounded by all kinds of super-duper electronic gadgets and software applications for organizing your life. Some are really clunky or inconvenient to use and you can easily forget where you've stored stuff and on what device. Pretty soon you'll need another organizer just to keep track of all your electronics. Even now you probably spend so much time using these methods that you don't actually *do* anything! So, what's the alternative?

**Use one method for your to-do list and stick to it!**

If you prefer using the standard pen and paper to make lists or reminders, then do so. At least you won't need batteries! If you love gadgets and spreadsheets, stick to using only one device or application. If you're using a computer, make sure you backup any important information!

**Keep a notebook handy**

Keep one of these in your pocket at all times, so you can jot down thoughts or tasks on the fly. You can then incorporate those notebook entries into your to-do lists.

**Do one thing at a time**

That's probably THE single most important piece of advice I can give you! Though the term 'multi-tasking' is all the rage at the moment (and it might impress your boss), you'll simply get confused or end up doing lots of things badly. Ok, it's not great to focus obsessively on one thing at the exclusion of others either, but by doing one task at a time, you can ensure quality and keep track of your projects.

**Find a good place for everything and keep it in its place**

My mom used to say this adage and I couldn't agree more! By 'place', I don't just mean in a box, shelf, or cupboard; I also mean room. Keep mugs in the kitchen, medicines in the bathroom, and toys in the 'playroom.'

**Keep it simple, stupid!**

Always, always think about what you are doing and ask yourself "Is this the easiest, simplest way?" If you're not sure – Wiki it, or buy a good book – check out my website judithturnbridge.com for some other great titles (sorry, I couldn't resist).

**Put it away after you've finished!**

Get into the habit of putting things away *immediately* after you use them. The best way to avoid clutter is to prevent the mess from building up in the first place.

**Tidy up along the way!**

As I said earlier, as soon as you see a mess, tidy up!

**Use color coded files**

You'll be amazed how such a simple innovation can change your life! There are many applications for this. For example, I keep all my outstanding bills in a red folder, all my paid ones in a blue folder, any outstanding invoices in a yellow folder, and the paid ones in a green folder. Through this I can see at a glance what needs to be paid and who owes me.

### Use a calendar, wipe boards, and bulletin boards

I covered the why and how on these earlier. But remember, whiteboards aren't just for work; they're a Godsend for the home, too. I've got one by the fridge, one in my study, and even one in the hall. The hallway one is particularly useful as it allows people to leave notes as they leave the house. Plus, it's a lot cheaper and quicker than texting! Make sure, however, you draw sections onto the boards, so they're not filled with a mass of meaningless words!

### Use colored notecards

Keep them on you at all times. Write individual tasks on them and throw them away as soon as the task is done. If you keep the cards in one of those plastic-lidded notecard boxes, you can then easily sort through them. This may seem an old-fashioned way of doing things, but it's an incredibly simple and cheap way of organizing your thoughts. And once again, no batteries!

### Have less stuff!

You'll have less clutter, less to worry about, less to go missing, less to go wrong, less to tidy, less to maintain, less to rely on, and less to organize if you get rid of the things you don't need. Oh, and did I mentioned, a lot more space?

### Don't be a control freak!

Learn to trust people with critical tasks in all areas of your life. Ask yourself why you may have a problem with this; is it because you feel superior, you've been badly let down in the past, or you're projecting your own sense of incompetence onto others? Whatever the reasons, challenge those views and ask yourself what the consequences of such behavior may be. Apart from being a pain in the butt to those around you, you'll be overworked and, of course, won't be able to learn better ways of doing things.

### Don't be afraid to ask for help

Some people, especially men, view asking for help as a sign of weakness and fear they will be looked upon as stupid or incompetent if they do. However, the stupid thing is NOT to ask for help when you need it or to pretend to understand something when you don't. Many people spend a lifetime pretending to cope, and most of them aren't fooling anyone; some of them may even wind up ill or even dead because of the stress from this!

**Just say no!**

Now, we get onto the topic of assertiveness. This is a big subject, but at the heart of it is simply knowing how to stick up for your 'rights' without suppressing the rights of others. Feeling confident enough to say 'no' is central to this. Many 'nice' people, especially women, feel guilty turning others down or worry they are perceived as unhelpful, rude, or lazy. Well – don't feel like that! Just say no! Not only do you have the 'right' to say no, by saying 'yes' to everything, you'll become swamped by tasks. Ultimately, you will fail to follow through on your previous commitments to people.

**Do it now!**

Stop wasting time thinking about it – put this book down and get on with it!

## And Finally...

We've made it to the end of our little odyssey and hopefully you've picked up some useful tips along the way. Now all you have to do is motivate yourself and put these tips into practice. Tell yourself it's time to say goodbye to a life of stressful chaos and hello to a world of ordered predictability (or something a lot less corny).

Mark your diary with the day and time you intend to begin putting your life in order and honor that deadline.

Regardless of how you do so, challenge yourself to change your sloppy ways, and then get off your behind and do it!

Lack of motivation is one of the biggest obstacles to overcome in life, and if I can be bothered, I might even write a book about this in future! Stay tuned readers – You 'aint seen nothin' yet!

# About the Author

Judith Turnbridge is a married artist with an interest in interior design. She enjoys painting, calligraphy, and caring for her garden. Her two children have now grown up and flown the nest, and the two hungry mouths she now feeds belong to her two fluffy cats.

Other books by Judith Turnbridge:

**Super Simple Home Cleaning:** The Best House Cleaning Tips for Green Cleaning the Home

**The Super Simple 30-Day Home Cleaning Plan:** Making Time to Beat the Grime

**How to Declutter Your Home for Simple Living:** Decluttering Tips and Closet Organization Ideas for Creating Your Own Personal Oasis

**Out of Sight, Out of Mind:** Easy Home Organization Tips and Storage Solutions for Clutter-Free Living

**Nature's Miracle Elixir:** The Essential Health Benefits of Coconut Oil

**How to Survive a Disaster:** Emergency Preparedness for You and Your Family

Printed in Great Britain
by Amazon